THE FATHER'S SONG

A COLLECTION OF VISUAL BIBLICAL MEDITATIONS
AROUND THE MEANING OF TRUE CHRISTMAS and ADVENT

SENT TO FRIENDS OVER MANY YEARS AND
DEDICATED TO FAMILY AND FRIENDS PAST, PRESENT AND FUTURE
ESPECIALLY MY MUM AND DAD, MY THREE BROTHERS AND THEIR FAMILIES
AND THE CLEMENTS AND HUMPHRIES:
'JEAN, HERE IS THE BOOK, AS PROMISED...'

"But there will be no more gloom for her who was in anguish....
The people that walk in darkness shall see a great Light;
Those who live in a dark land, the Light will shine on them...
For a Child will be born to us, a Son will be given to us,
And the government will rest on His shoulders;
And His name will be called
Wonderful Counsellor, Mighty God, Eternal Father, Prince of Peace..."
Isaiah Chapter 9 verses 1-7

IMMANUEL

GOD WITH US

How DID this book grow?

Well, it was inspired by other artists who made a special 'work' each year to show forth a God-given heart-thought and sent it out to friends at Christmas and New Year... and I was given a very large drawing book... so this became the home for my yearly visit to the paradox of the Saviour King cradled in an animal's feeding trough about 2000 years ago.

So, over the years, late November, or even early December, is the time to set aside waiting time, no matter how busy at work or home, listen to 'Young Messiah' (Thank you Helen) and ask the Lord "What next?" Sometimes the focus was the Child and prophetic words from scripture, sometimes a Carol or a theme : shepherds, angels, kings, the heavenly Hosts and more recently meditations on the majestic beginnings of John's Gospel and thus Genesis, the book of all beginnings.

There is an awareness of the significance of scripture, always...so the Word is woven in and out and through each biblical visual meditation.
Sometimes children pop into the sketches and scribbles. (Apart from one or two, they are all rough jottings of thoughts)... children from current news of crises in the world and in Israel. Family members are hidden there too! They are brought to the Stable.

When as ready as possible, the yearly visit to Copyprint in Bromley was fitted in and card selected for printing, envelopes and stamps bought and the task begun of sending out to family, friends, and any I hoped would appreciate them... as my gift to the Saviour, my way of making Him known, whether He came in December or the Biblical Autumn festivals. It was simply to tell His story as best I could and honour His Name: Jesus, God is Saviour (Yeshua in Hebrew), Immanuel, God with us.

My big book is nearly full now, and colour developed in many of the black and white originals, but they can go on another journey: with you, dear reader, in this new book, 'The Father's Song.'

Make it your own. Add your own notes and references. Journal with children, point and tell, look up the bible verses, sing worship songs and carols. May this book be used to bless the celebrations of the birth of the King: the King who has come and will come again; the first time in a hidden way, but next time in clouds of Glory!
God has promised... and He keeps His Word!

Christine M. The Feast of Tabernacles, October 2012

SOME WAYS OF WORKING WITH THIS BOOK:
* Ask questions such as: What can I see in the image? Note them down. * What words or text; what pictures or symbols? * Do you think the colours are significant? * Make notes on the text page opposite, your thoughts or other verses. Look up any new words.
* Why not try drawing shapes round some of the text passages, perhaps a tree shape, or maybe a star or a dove.
* You could decorate each text page and add colour, especially in the first part of the book. * Be creative!

Beginnings

'In the beginning
GOD Created
the Heavens
and
the Earth.
And the earth
was without form,
and void:
and darkness
was upon
the face of the deep
And the Spirit of GOD
was hovering upon the face
of the waters.
And GOD said:
"LET THERE BE
LIGHT!"
And there was Light.
And GOD saw the Light
that it was good;
And GOD
divided the Light
from
the Darkness.
And GOD called the Light
"DAY"
and the darkness
He called
"NIGHT".
And the evening and the morning were the First Day.'

Genesis chapter 1 verse 1-5

The Gospel of John chapter 1 v 1

'In the beginning was the WORD,
and the WORD was with God
and the WORD was God.
He was in the beginning with God.
All things came into being by Him,
and apart from Him
nothing came into being that has come into being.'

Colossians chapter 1
Verses 15....17

Paul the Apostle writes about Jesus:

"...Who is the image of the invisible God, the first-born of
every creature:
for by Him all things were created...
that are in heaven, and that are in earth,
visible, and invisible,
whether thrones, or dominions
or principalities or powers:
and He is before all things
and by Him all things consist (hold together)."

IN THE BEGINNING ~ GOD CREATED th HEAVENS AND THE EARTH ~ AND IT WAS GOOD. GENESIS ch.1

Light

'Then God said:
"Let there be light!"
and there was light.
And God saw that the light was good
And God separated the light
from the darkness.
And God called the light 'Day'
And the darkness He called 'Night'.

And there was evening and there was
morning
The First Day.'

Genesis
chapter 1
verses 3-5

'In The Beginning Was The Word'

'In Him was Life
and the Life was the light of man
and the Light shines in the darkness
and
the darkness
did not
overcome (or understand) it.'

The Gospel of John
chapter 1
verses 4-5

> IN THE BEGINNING WAS THE WORD AND THE WORD WAS WITH GOD · THE WORD WAS GOD

Firmaments

'Then God said:
"Let there be a firmament
in the midst of the waters
and let it separate
the waters from the waters."
And God made the firmament
and separated the waters from the
waters which were
above the firmament
and it was so.
And God called the firmament
"Heaven"
And there was evening
and there was morning
Day Two.'

Genesis chapter 1 verses 6-8

What is a firmament?

Try looking it up in a dictionary, or maybe a
Bible dictionary or even a Concordance.
I use a Young's Concordance because it gives the
Hebrew or Greek version of a word, and
sometimes you can discover hidden meanings,
lost in translation.
In my Young's Concordance, the Hebrew for
'Firmament' is *raqia*, or expanse.
You could go out and look up into the night sky
to get some idea of what it might look like,
especially on a clear
star lit night.

IN THE BEGINNING WAS THE WORD AND THE WORD WAS WITH GOD ✝ THE WORD WAS GOD

Fruit And Seeds

'Then God said
"Let the waters below the heavens be
gathered into one place
and let the dry land appear."
And it was so.
and God called the dry land 'earth'
and the gathering of the waters
He called 'seas'.
and God saw that it was good.
Then God said :
"Let the earth sprout vegetation;
plants yielding seed and fruit trees bearing
fruit after their kind with seed in them,
in the earth."
and it was so.
And the earth brought forth vegetation,
plants yielding seed after their kind and
trees bearing fruit with seed in them
after their kind.
And God saw that it was good.
and there was evening and there was
morning, Day Three.'

Genesis chapter 1 verses 9-13

Fruit And Seeds

'In the beginning was the Word
and the Word was with God
and the Word was God...
all things came into being
through Him...'

John's Gospel Ch 1 verses 1-3

'A body Thou hast prepared for Me'

Hebrews Ch 10 v 5; Psalm 40 vv 6-9

'That which you sow,
you do not sow the body which is to be but a
bare grain, perhaps of wheat or of something
else, but God gives it a body just as He
wished, and to each of the seeds
a body of its own...
...so also is the resurrection of the dead. It is
sown a perishable body, it is raised an
imperishable body, it is sown in dishonour, it
is raised in glory; it is sown in weakness, it is
raised in power; it is sown a natural body it
is raised a spiritual body.
so also it is written: "The first man, Adam,
became a living soul."
the last Adam
became a Life-giving Spirit...'

1 Corinthians chapter 15 verses 35-49

IN THE BEGINNING WAS THE WORD AND THE WORD WAS WITH GOD · THE WORD WAS GOD

Lights

'Then God said:
"Let there be lights in the firmament of
the heavens
to separate the day from the night,
and let them be for signs and for seasons
and for days and for years.
and let them be for lights in the
firmament of the heavens to give light on
the earth."
And it was so.
And God made the two great lights:
the greater to govern the day
and the lesser to govern the night.
He made the stars also
and God placed them in the firmament
of the heavens to give light on the earth
and to govern the day and the night
and to separate
the light from the darkness.
And God saw that it was good
and there was evening
and there was morning
Day Four.'

Genesis
chapter 1
verses 14-19

The Light

Jesus said:
"I AM the Light of the World.
whoever follows Me
shall not walk in darkness
but
shall have the Light of Life."

The Gospel of John
chapter 8
verse 12

✷

'See, amid the winter's snow
Born for us on earth below,
See, the tender Lamb appears,
Promised from eternal years!

Hail, thou ever blessed morn!
Hail Redemption's happy dawn!
Sing through all Jerusalem,
Christ is born in Bethlehem!

**Lo! Within a manger lies
He Who built the starry skies,
He, Who 'throned in height sublime,
Sits amid the cherubim!'**

Carol by Edward Caswell (1814-1878)

IN THE BEGINNING WAS THE WORD AND THE WORD WAS WITH GOD · THE WORD WAS GOD

Life

'And God said:

"Let the waters
team with swarms of living creatures,
and let birds fly above the earth
in the open expanse of the heavens."
And God created great sea monsters
and every living creature that moves
with which the waters swarmed
after their kind
and every winged bird
after its kind.
And God saw that it was good.
And God blessed them
saying:
"Be fruitful and multiply,
and fill the waters in the seas
And let birds multiply on the earth."
And there was evening
and there was morning
Day Five.'

Genesis
chapter 1
verses 20-23

Life

Jesus, the Word of God:
'All things came into being by Him
and apart from Him
nothing came into being
that has come into being.
In Him was Life
And the Life was the Light of men.'

John's Gospel
chapter 1
verses 3-4

IN THE BEGINNING WAS THE WORD AND THE WORD WAS WITH GOD · THE WORD WAS GOD

Man And Beast

'Then God said:
"Let the earth bring forth living creatures
after their kind,
and creeping things, and beasts of the earth
after their kind."
and it was so.
And God made the beasts of the earth
after their kind
and the cattle after their kind
and every thing that creeps on the ground
after its kind.
And God saw that it was good.
And God said;
"Let us make man in Our image,
according to Our likeness,
And let them rule over the fish of the sea
And over the birds of the sky
And over the cattle
And over all the earth
And over every creeping thing
that creeps on the earth."
And God created man in His own image,
in the image of God He created him;
male and female He created them.
And God blessed them"

*Genesis
chapter 1
verses 24-28*

'And God said to them:
"Be fruitful and multiply
And fill the earth and subdue it
And rule over the fish of the sea
And over the birds of the sky
And over every living thing
that moves on the earth."
Then God said:
"Behold ,
I have given you
every plant yielding seed
that is on the surface of all the earth
and every tree which has fruit yielding seed,
it shall be food for you.
and to every beast of the earth
and to every bird of the sky
and to everything that moves on the earth
which has life I have given
every green plant for food."

And it was so.
And God saw all that He had made,
And behold, it was very good.
And there was evening
and there was morning, Day Six.'

*Genesis
chapter 1
verses 29-31*

IN THE BEGINNING WAS THE WORD AND THE WORD WAS WITH GOD & THE WORD WAS GOD

Sabbath Rest

'Thus
the heavens
and the earth
were completed
and all their hosts
and by the seventh day
God completed His work
which He had done.

And He rested on the seventh day

from all His work which He had done
then God blessed the seventh day
and sanctified it
because in it He rested from all His work
which God had created and made.'

Genesis chapter 2 verses 1-3

Psalm 8

'O Lord our Lord,
how majestic is your name in all the earth'
who hast displayed Thy splendour
above the heavens! ...
When I consider the heavens,
the work of Thy fingers,
the moon and the stars,
which Thou hast ordained;
what is man that Thou art mindful of him,
and the son of man,
that Thou dost care for him?
Yet Thou hast made him a little lower than
God, and dost crown him with glory and
majesty!
Thou dost make him to rule
over the works of Thy hands;
Thou dost put all things under his feet, all
sheep and oxen, and also the beasts of the
field, the birds of the heavens
and the fish of the sea and whatever passes
through the paths of the seas.
O Lord our Lord,
How majestic is Your name
in all the earth!'

**see also 1 Corinthians chapter 15
and Hebrews chapter 2 verses 5-18**

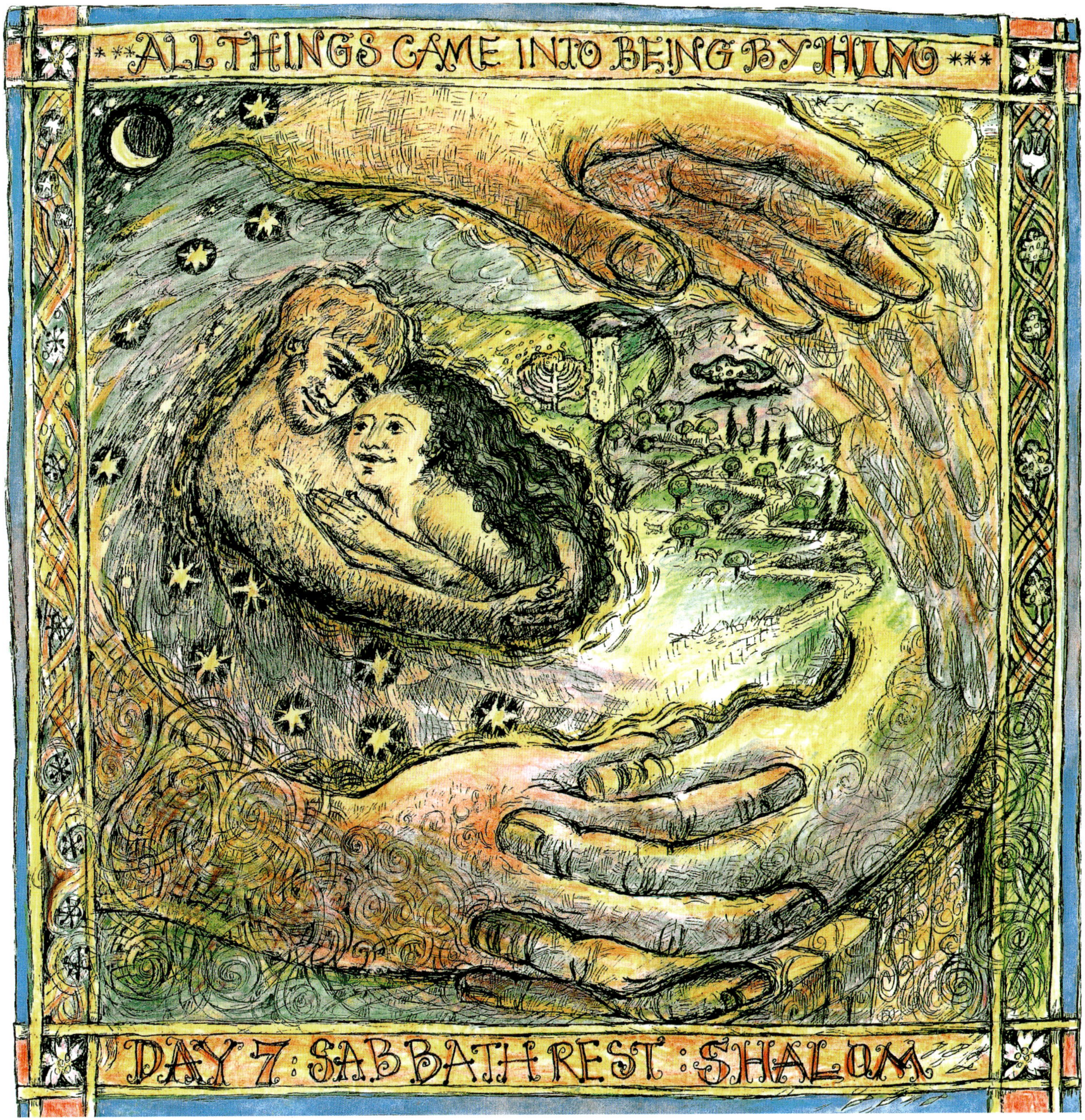
ALL THINGS CAME INTO BEING BY HIM
DAY 7 : SABBATH REST : SHALOM

Blue Wings: Thoughts

David sang to the Lord:

"Where can I go from Thy Spirit?
or where can I flee from Thy presence?
if I ascend to heaven, Thou art there;
if I make my bed in Sheol, behold,
Thou art there.
if I take the wings of the dawn,
if I dwell in the remotest part of the sea,
even there Thy hand will lead me
and Thy right hand will lay hold of me.
if I say, "Surely the darkness
will overwhelm me,
and the light around me will be night,"
even the darkness is not dark to Thee,
and the night is bright as the day.
Darkness and light
are alike to Thee."

Psalm 139 verses 7-12

Of Boaz, The Redeemer Kinsman And Ancestor of Jesus, son of David

Ruth said to him:
"Cover me with the wings of your garment for you are my redeemer kinsman." (In other words, take me under your covering protection as wife.)

See Ruth chapter 3 verse 9

Shelter

'He who dwells in the shelter of the Most High
will abide in the shadow of the Almighty.
I will say to the Lord: "My refuge and my
fortress, my God in whom I trust!"
for it is He who delivers you
from the snare of the trapper,
and from the deadly pestilence.
He will cover you with His pinions
and under His wings you may seek refuge;
His faithfulness is a shield and a bulwark.

Psalm 91 verses 1-4

Zechariah's Prophecy of The Dayspring from on High

"And you, child, will be called the prophet of
the Most High for you will go on
before the Lord to prepare His ways,
to give to His people
the knowledge of salvation by the forgiveness of
their sins because
of the tender mercy of our God
whereby the Day Spring from on high has
visited us, to shine upon those who sit in
darkness and the shadow of death, to guide our
feet into the way of peace."

Luke chapter 1 verses 68-79

·in·HIM·was·LIFE+the·LIFE·
·was·the·LIGHT·of·men·
THE·LIGHT·shines
·in·the·DARKNESS···
ALL·THINGS·WERE·CREATED·THROUGH·HIM·
+APART·FROM·HIM·NOTHING·CAME·INTO·BEING
THAT·HAS·COME·INTO·BEING

The Fall And The Promise

ANCC 1979

Lost from God
driven out.
Yearning forever
after what has been
forever lost...
through disobedience,
not trusting God's word
and believing lies.
Lost fellowship with God
for which they had been first created;
for them now no purpose,
no hope apart from Him
and His mercy.
Mercy; mercy only
from a just God who
Holy is and keeps His word,
both cursing and blessing.
Anguish in the heart of God..
the heart of love who is Love
and holiness and
justice in one.
How we hurt Him
when first we turned away,
and believed the liar
and father of lies,
instead of Him
and caused Him then
to banish those He made
to share the joy of His creation,
to share His heart's love,
to know Him.
"Mercy!" "Mercy!"
only was their cry,
stumbling away,
hearts shrivelled to emptiness.
Now loss of joy and peace,
dead towards Him
who was once their
heart's desire.
Rebellion needs must end in
estrangement, bitterness,
death to love and trust and innocence;
End of hope
apart from knowledge
of the nature of Him
they had sinned against
so grievously.
BUT hope He gave that day,
when anguish torn
the two left Him.
Hope of One, Who,
born of woman
would bruise that
serpent satan's head
and destroy his
power and hold over
man forever.
One, who, mercy,
Saviour God by name
would come to redeem...
to buy back
what had become
worthless...
paying the price,
being that price
Himself.

...and the darkness... did not overpower it...

Jesus The Branch The Key of David The Root

Thorn Crown: The Father's Song

*"Behold My Servant will prosper,
He will be high and lifted up,
and greatly exalted.
Just as many were astonished at you my people,
So His appearance was marred
more than any man,
And His form more than the sons of men.
Thus He will sprinkle many nations;
Kings will shut their mouths
on account of Him;
For what had not been told them they will see,
And what they had not heard
they will understand..."*

Isaiah Ch 52
vv 13-14

The Prophet's Song

*"For He grew up before Him like a tender shoot,
and like a root out of parched ground;
He has no stately form or majesty
that we should look on Him.
nor appearance
that we should be attracted to Him.
He was despised and forsaken of men,
a man of sorrows and acquainted with grief;
and like one from whom men hide their face,
He was despised, and we did not esteem Him.
Surely our sickness He Himself bore,
and our sorrows He carried;
yet we ourselves esteemed Him stricken,
smitten of God and afflicted,
but He was pierced through for our transgressions,
He was crushed for our iniquities;
the chastening for our well-being fell upon Him,
and by His scourging we are healed
all of us like sheep have gone astray
each of us has turned to his own way; but the Lord
has caused the iniquity of us all
to fall on Him."*

see Isaiah
Ch 53 vv 1-12

The Servant's Song:

Jesus said : this is about Me:
*"The Spirit of the Lord God is upon Me
Because He has anointed Me
To bring good news to the afflicted;
He has sent Me to bind up the broken-hearted,
To proclaim liberty to captives,
And freedom to prisoners;
To proclaim the favourable year of the Lord,
And the day of vengeance of our God;
To comfort all who mourn,
To grant those who mourn in Zion,
Giving them a garland instead of ashes,
The oil of gladness instead of mourning,
The mantle of praise instead of a spirit of fainting,
So they will be called oaks of righteousness,
The planting of the Lord, that He may be glorified."*

Isaiah Ch 61 vv 1-4...
and Luke Ch 4 vv 17-21

The Blood of the Lamb Slain from
Before the Foundation of the World.

The Promise

"Blessed is she who believed that there would be a fulfilment of what had been spoken to her by the Lord!"

For many years this verse has shone out to me as an encouragement to trust God in a way almost separate from its original context: the annunciation and conception of Jesus, Son of God, Saviour of the world.

It was like a challenge to believe God in opposition to the apparent realities of every day life; a promise to be received and a trust to be held because of the character of the Promise Maker: the Lord God through Whom all things were created. In life there is a call to pray, trust, believe, hope, have faith… and act in the light of this promise, sometimes even when all seems hopeless, helpless, and dark.

"Faith is the substance of things hoped for, the conviction of things not seen, for by it men of old gained approval."

see Hebrews Ch 11 verse 1-2.

Whose approval? God's approval.

Father God loves faith in His children and He looks for it as we look for ripe fruit on a tree. It is a source of great rejoicing, to see His childrens' loving and expectant trust in His character, His trustworthy promises. He loves to hear His children echo the prayer Jesus gave as our pattern:

"May Thy kingdom come and Thy will be done on earth as it is in heaven."

see Luke 11, vv 1-4.

His will is good and perfect and loving, His kingdom rule is that of loving kindness, mercy, justice and truth.

In Genesis, the book of beginnings, we are told that God spoke the word and it was done. All Creation was good and very pleasing to Him. Loving kindness, mercy, justice and truth were the rule.

In the New Testament John's Gospel tells us this Word is Jesus, who was in the beginning with God, and that all things came into being through Him. "Apart from Him nothing came into being that has come into being." see John 1 verses 1-5

Imagine this Beginning, when all was complete and fresh and new and pristine: no harm or hurt or pain or tears or heart break: just joy and love and work to do in harmony with Father God, who loved to walk and talk with the caretakers of His estate: the man and the woman. Their work was to govern and care and people the place He had made for them.

All creation must have trembled to see this kingdom rule established under the Father's authority, for His loving decision was to give them freedom to choose: His way or their way. And He spelled out the consequences: 'These trees, not that tree, all this, but not that, life or death: the garden or the wilderness.' Made in the image of God: to will, to decide to believe or not believe that He would keep His promise.

The Hebrew Scriptures tells how the man and the woman chose not to trust God's word to them, and instead, believe the lies of the serpent. As a result, the world as we know it came into being: still amazing, but now mixed with fear, tears, struggle, separation from God, and ultimately, death. Yet, even as they lost the right to the Tree of Life and life in the precious garden of delight, the Lord God promised them a Redeemer: One day, a man born of woman would come and deal the death blow to the head of this deceiver, the adversary of God and mankind. The One to come would pay the price to bring the whole of Creation back under God's authority.

The Promise Kept.

Now here we have a young Hebrew woman of the house of Judah, brought up to expect God to fulfil His Promise that one day, through the seed of Abraham and Sarah, "all the families of the earth shall be blessed." see Genesis 12 verses2-3.

She knew that this was partially fulfilled, because Abraham and Sarah eventually had one son, Isaac. Through Isaac came Jacob, and Jacob's twelve sons became heads of the twelve tribes of Israel.

As God had said would happen to Abraham, before Isaac was even conceived, Jacob and his family went down to Egypt and eventual slavery for a period of about four hundred years. Then they were redeemed by God's intervention, set free and eventually moved into the Promised Land.

Generations later Mary, (Miriam in Hebrew), would celebrate God's promise of help at every festival, every year: Passover, Pentecost, Trumpets, Yom Kippor, Tabernacles and Hannukah. There was a Deliverer yet to come: year by year her people still prayed for Messiah to come: the Anointed One who would somehow complete the Promised redemption: He would legally buy back the whole earth for God.

"Maybe THIS year Messiah will come"

"It will come clear when Messiah comes"

" Lord, save us! Send Messiah! Hosannah!"

And so He comes .Unexpectedly. Quietly.

When no-one is looking. And in humility, poverty, obscurity… This time.

Only a few were still listening and looking and hoping for God to keep His Promise, but still, they were there and came and saw and wondered how this thing could be: that God the Word would come Himself and, wrapped in humanity, live (or tabernacle) among us for a while.

He would be the Door back to the Father, to the Tree of Life and the Garden relationship with Our Creator.

He would keep faith with the Father's Promise by dying in our place on a tree, so that all who trust in the promise may walk free, healed and restored.

NB   There is another promise yet to be kept:

The Bible tells us that Messiah Jesus will return one day,

but then it will be in power and great glory,

as King of Kings and Lord of Lords.

see Luke Ch 21 verses25-27; Mark Ch 13 verses 24-27; Acts Ch 1 verses 9-11

God so loved the world, that He gave His only Son, that whoever believes on Him should not perish but have everlasting Life — John 3 v 16

IN THE BEGINNING GOD CREATED THE HEAVENS AND THE EARTH GENESIS ch 1 v 1

"MAY IT BE TO ME AS YOU HAVE SAID"

JOHN'S GOSPEL ch 1 v 1-14

'IN THE BEGINNING WAS THE WORD AND THE WORD WAS WITH GOD AND THE WORD WAS GOD. HE WAS IN THE BEGINNING WITH GOD. ALL THINGS CAME INTO BEING THROUGH HIM AND APART FROM HIM NOTHING CAME INTO BEING THAT HAS COME INTO BEING. IN HIM WAS LIFE AND THE LIFE WAS THE LIGHT OF MEN. ... AND THE WORD BECAME FLESH AND DWELT [or TABERNACLED] AMONG US; AND WE BEHELD HIS GLORY, GLORY AS OF THE ONLY BEGOTTEN FROM THE FATHER, FULL OF GRACE + TRUTH"

Luke Chapter 1 v 26-79

Now in the sixth month the angel Gabriel was sent from God to a city in Galilee, called Nazareth, to a virgin engaged to a man who's name was Joseph, of the descendants of David; and the virgin's name was Mary (Miriam). And coming in he said to her, "Hail favoured one! The Lord is with you."

But she was greatly troubled at this statement, and kept pondering what kind of salutation this might be.

And the angel said to her, "Do not be afraid, Mary; for you have found favour with God. And behold, you will conceive in your womb, and bear a Son, and you will name Him Jesus. He will be great, and will be called the Son of the Most High; and the Lord God will give Him the throne of His father David; and He will reign over the house of Jacob forever; and His kingdom will have no end."

And Mary said to the angel, "How can this be since I am a virgin?"

And the angel answered her and said to her, "The Holy Spirit will come upon you, and the power of the Most High will overshadow you; and for that reason the holy offspring shall be called the Son of God.", even your cousin Elizabeth has also conceived a son in her old age; and she who was called barren is now in her sixth month. For nothing will be impossible with God."

And Mary said, " Behold the bond slave of the Lord; be it done to me according to your word." And the angel departed from her.

Mary goes straight to see her cousin Elizabeth and...

Elizabeth, on meeting Mary cries out: "...And blessed is she who believed that there would be a fulfilment of what was spoken to her by the Lord!"

And Mary declared:

"My soul exalts the Lord, and my spirit has rejoiced in God my Saviour, ... for the Mighty One has done great things for me; and holy is His name...."

Zechariah prophesies over his son John the Baptist:

'Blessed be the Lord God of Israel, for He has visited us and accomplished redemption for His people, and has raised up a horn of salvation for us in the House of David His servant..."

"and you, child, will be called the prophet of the Most High; for you will go on before the Lord to prepare His ways; to give His people the knowledge of salvation by the forgiveness of their sins, because of the tender mercy of our God, with which the Dayspring from on high shall visit us; to shine upon those who sit in darkness and the shadow of death, to guide our feet into the way of peace."

Song

Advent Carol

O come O come Emmanuel!
And ransom captive Israel,
That mourns in lonely exile here
Until the Son of God appear.
Rejoice, rejoice! Emmanuel
Shall come to thee, O Israel.

O come, O come Thou Lord of Might,
Who to Thy tribes, on Sinai's height,
In ancient times, didst give The Law
In cloud and majesty and awe.
Rejoice, rejoice! Emmanuel
Shall come to thee, O Israel!

O Come, Thou Rod of Jesse, free
Thine own from satan's tyranny;
From depths of hell Thy people save
And give them victory o'er the grave.
Rejoice, rejoice! Emmanuel
Shall come to thee, O Israel!

O Come, Thou Dayspring, come and cheer
Our spirits by Thine Advent here;
Disperse the gloomy clouds of night
And death's dark shadows put to flight.
Rejoice, rejoice! Emmanuel
Shall come to thee, O Israel!

O come, Thou Key of David, come
And open wide our heavenly home;
Make safe the Way that leads on high
And close the path to misery.
Rejoice, rejoice! Emmanuel
Shall come to thee, O Israel!

From the Latin (12th century) tr: John Mason Neale (1818-66)
Emmanuel means 'God with us'

POINTS TO PONDER

*Look at each verse and ask yourself what is being said there eg:
*What does Emmanuel mean? *What is a ransom and who is Israel? Why are they captive?
*Who is being asked to come and rescue? * Who is the Son of God? and *What is verse two about?
* Is the Rod of Jesse a plant or a tree or a twig? Would a concordance help? Try Isaiah Ch 11 v 1 *There's a lot about dark shadows, death and dying. What does that mean for you?

Try looking at Isaiah Ch 25 vv 6-9 and 1 Corinthians Ch 15 for a start.

*What's a 'Dayspring': The morning star? The dawn? * What does 'Advent' mean? *What significance could this have for you?
*Who is the 'Key of David', and why 'David'? Can this be found in the scriptures? try Isaiah Ch22 v22 and Revelation Ch 3 v7. Who or what is 'The Way' to Life? John Ch 14
Have you met Him yet? He loves you
THAT MUCH!
Is this the Father's Song?

IN·HIM·WAS·LIFE · THE·LIFE·WAS·THE·LIGHT·OF·MEN · THE·LIGHT·SHINES·IN·THE·DARKNESS · THE·DARKNESS·DID·NOT·OVERPOWER·IT

IN THE BEGINNING WAS THE WORD and the WORD was with GOD — Glory to GOD in the highest heaven · every eye shall see Him · every tongue proclaiming Jesus the Messiah is LORD

The Father's Celebration

In the Middle East fathers celebrate the birth of a son
by inviting all the neighbours to a party, with music, great joy and thanksgiving.

So, at the birth of His Son,
The Almighty God and Everlasting Father sent His servant, the angel Gabriel,
to announce the good news to poor, terrified shepherds
as they watched over the sacrificial flocks of sheep
in the open fields around Bethlehem.

What did they think?
How did they react?*
...when they saw the myriads of angels crowding the sky
as they sang and watched and worshipped!
and what did the Father Himself think
as He looked down through the heavenly hosts
to the scene below...!

Luke's Gospel
Chapter 2
verses 8-20

*Look at the shepherds. They are reacting in different ways to the angel's message. Do you identify with any? Or would your reaction be different if you had been there? Try and put yourself in their place!

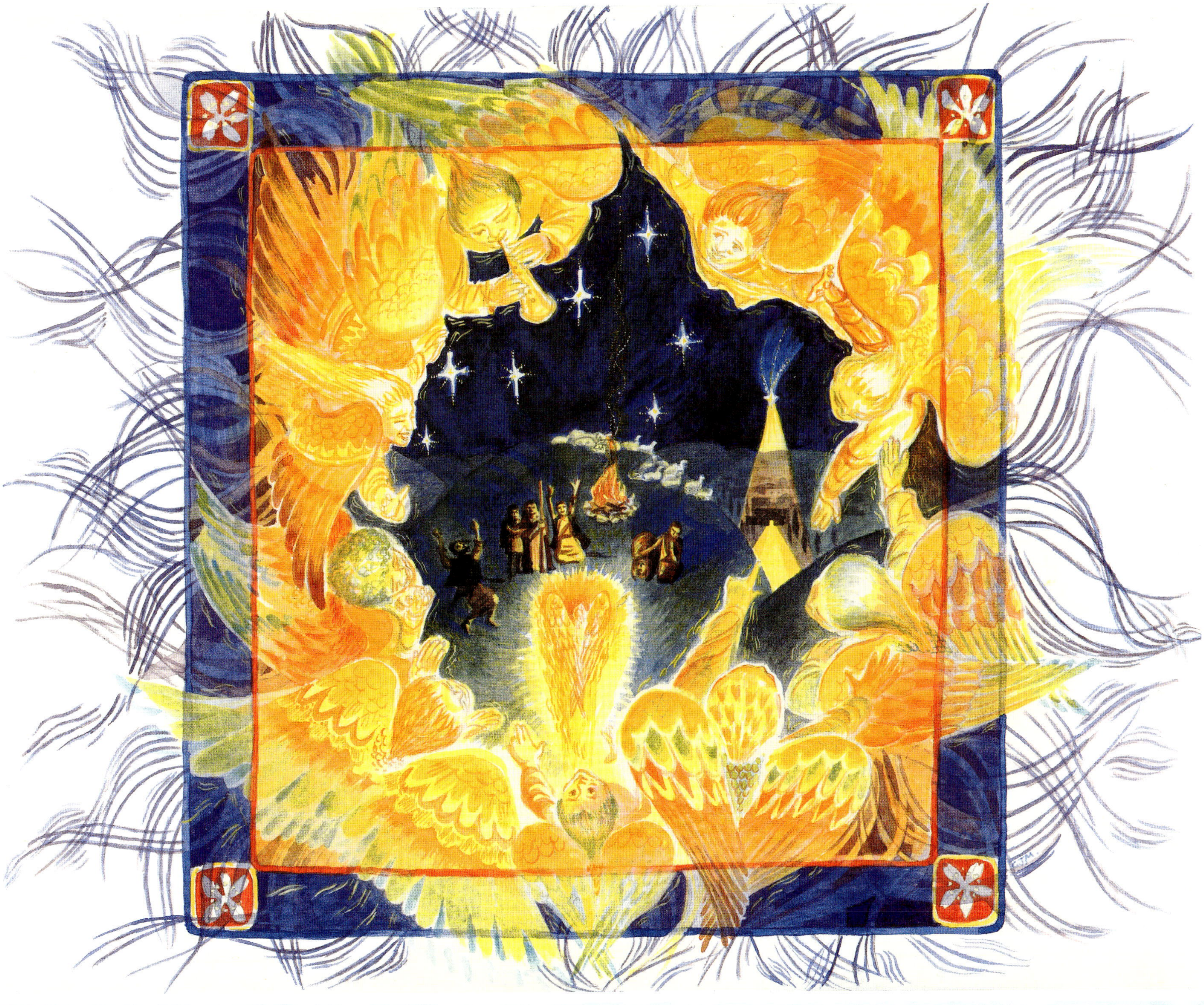

The Father's Light

In haste, the shepherds found their way there.
Was this where the Son of Almighty God Himself had been born?
... this rough shack, this animal shelter?
Above, on the roof-top, exhausted Jewish families, newly arrived in Bethlehem for the
Roman census, sleep on, unaware of the amazing event that had taken place so near.
One day, however, they too will wake up and join in with the shepherds...
Breathlessly, the rough men knock and wait.
A boy had thought to bring a lamb for a gift. You need a gift for a new-born.
At last, quietly the low door opens. Light floods out, chasing away the dark...
Low murmurs, a gentle welcome from deep inside,
and one by one, the men and boy stoop low to enter. Such joy. Such peace...
Who would have thought it...and everything just as the angel said.

After that night, everywhere they went, the shepherds told the story:
"The King is among us: He is even called 'Immanuel', 'God with us'!
The Father Himself invited us to join the celebration.
Come, see for yourself; wake up and don't delay...
It's the Father's Light we saw!"

Luke's Gospel
Chapter 2
verses 8-20

If you were in this picture, where would you be? Asleep? Searching and expecting to see Him? Or hiding, not sure of a welcome?

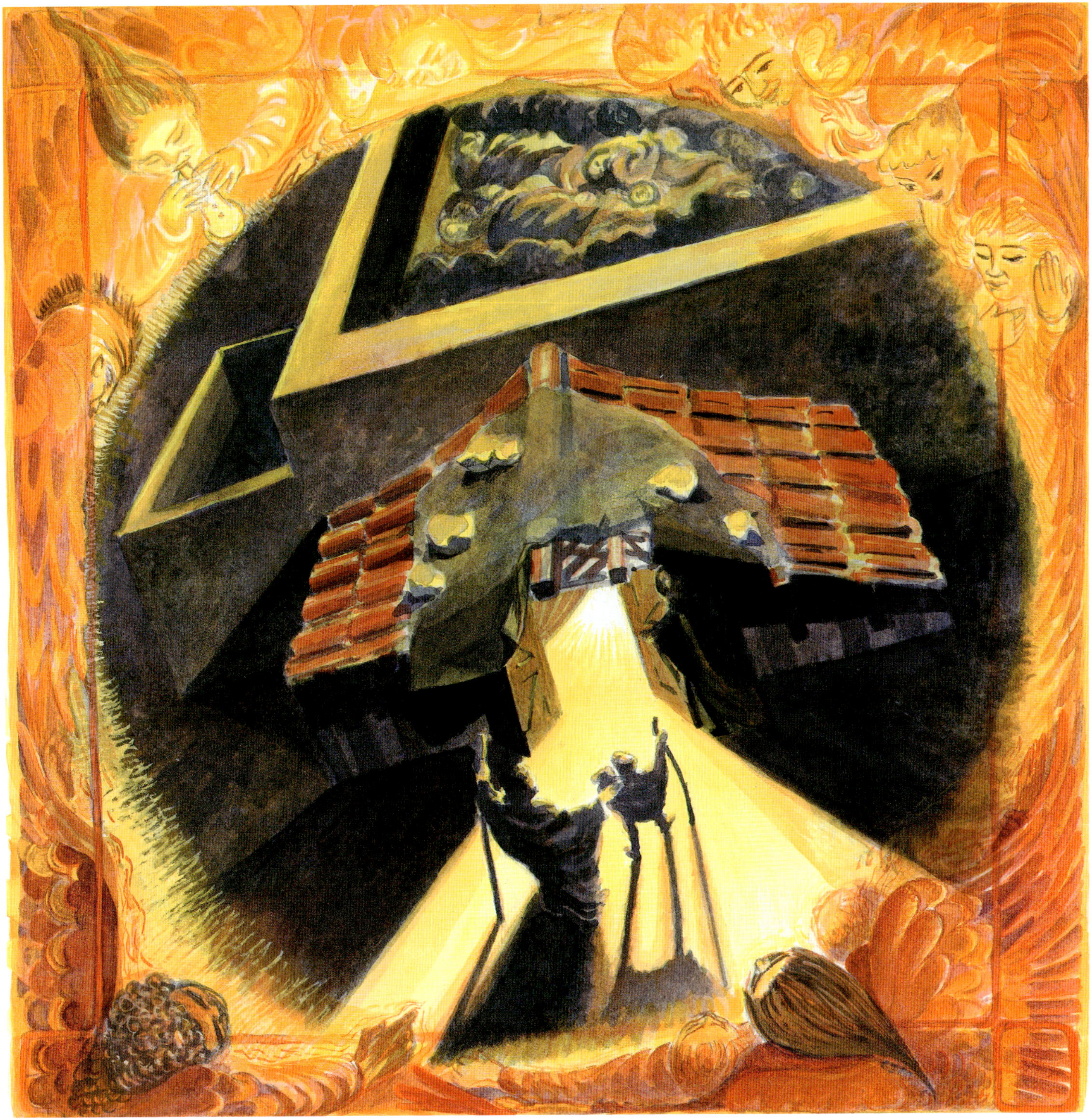

Word of God
Creator of the Universe
Mighty God
Prince of Peace
King of Kings
Lord of Lords
Wonder Counsellor
Everlasting Father
Adonai Eloheinu
El Shaddai
Son of God
Son of David
Son of Man
Messiah
The Lamb of God that Takes Away the Sin of the World

And she wrapped Him in swaddling cloths & laid Him in a manger

'Those who live in a dark land, The Light will shine on them.'

Isaiah chapter 9 verse 2

'Glory to God in the highest, and on earth peace among men with whom He is pleased.'

Luke chapter 2 verse 14

'Blessed is the King Who comes in the Name of The Lord!'

Luke chapter 19 verse 38

'The people who walk in darkness will see a Great Light.'

Isaiah chapter 9 verse 2

"For to us a CHILD is BORN, to us a SON is GIVEN, and the government will be on HIS shoulders, and HE will be called WONDERFUL COUNSELLOR, MIGHTY GOD, EVERLASTING FATHER, PRINCE of PEACE..."

ISAIAH 9 v.6

HAllelujah! Christ-Mas 1994 from Christine

"Receive the Kingdom like a child — like trust in me & become like one of these"

"Blessed are the pure in heart for they shall see God!"

O come & worship Christ~ the new born King!

Luke 18 v.16

From Christine ♡ 10/1/00 ~ shalom!

The Father's Door

At the end of time,
we may look back and see, by faith,
all the millions of men and women, boys and girls
from every tribe and tongue and nation who humbled themselves
and joined the shepherds as they made their way
to the Light of the World:
to Jesus, Son of God, Saviour,
The Lamb of God
born to take away the sin of a desperately needy world.

So I put them in,
streaming towards the light with hope in their hearts,
just like the shepherds.
Had not God Himself told them the good news
that would shake the world for all eternity?

Are you there?

Is there anyone you long for
to come out of the darkness and join you?
Why not be like the shepherds and tell,
share the glad song they heard that night:

*"Glory to God in the highest,
and on earth,
peace to men on whom His favour rests."*

Luke's Gospel
chapter 2
verses 30-32

"...For my eyes have seen your salvation, which you have prepared in the sight of all people, a light for revelation to the Gentiles and for glory to your people Israel." LUKE 9 v.30-32

"...there will be no more gloom for those who were in distress...; The people walking in darkness have seen a Great Light. On those living in the Land of the Shadow of Death a Light has dawned!" ISAIAH ch.9 v.1-2

*The first Adam
Of the earth, earthy.
Moulded from earth by God's hands;
In – breathed by God's breath
To become A living soul,
Natural man,
of the earth,*

*now fallen,
perishable,
corruptible.*

*see Genesis Ch 2 verse 7
1 Corinthians Ch 15 verse 45-48*

ALL THINGS CAME INTO BEING BY HIM

DAY 7: SABBATH REST : SHALOM

*The Last Adam
from heaven.
Life – giving Spirit,
Eternal and
Incorruptible;
Our Kinsman
Our Redeemer...
Born to buy us back
from Death's grip;
To swallow Death up
and breathe into Adam's children
His Breath,
His Spirit,
His Life.*

*See 1 Corinthians Ch 15
Isaiah Ch 25 verses 6-9*

IMMANU EL

GOD WITH US

The Father's Joy

Key Thoughts

The Holy of Holies,
Cherubim wings meeting
over the Mercy Seat.
El Shaddai:

✶ ✶ ✶

The Servant Light
from whom all other
lights must be lit.
The humility of
the Servant King.
Angelic hosts descending in
their myriads
to celebrate the coming of
the King of Kings with the
Shepherds
as they watch over the
sacrificial flocks outside
Bethlehem
(sleeping still).

✶ ✶ ✶

The Menorah,
like a lamp-stand
and like a tree…
Almond blossoms:
God is watching
over His Word
to perform it.
(Spring IS near)…
The Menorah,
of which the Lamp in
Tabernacle and Temple are
but a shadow of the True.

✶ ✶ ✶

Prophesies fulfilled and
Songs of Praise and
Adoration ascending.

✶ ✶ ✶

The Prayer Shawl of the
Father's Love
wrapped around the earth.
Law and Grace are met
together
in this
Tiny Child,
nursing at
His mother's breast:
fully human,
fully God.
Humility
Incarnate.

✶ ✶ ✶

All things ready to be
wrapped up
as a garment,
Ready
to be folded and put away,
in preparation
for the New Heaven
and the New Earth.

✶ ✶ ✶

Amen
12th December 1999

HIS GLORY, GLORY AS OF THE ONLY-BEGOTTEN OF THE FATHER: FULL OF GRACE AND TRUTH

IMMANUEL-GOD WITH US; SAVIOUR

AND THE WORD WAS MADE FLESH AND DWELT AMONG US: AND WE BEHELD

A Body Thou hast prepared for Me

BLESSED IS HE WHO COMES IN THE NAME OF THE LORD · BARUCH HA BA B'SHEM
בָּרוּךְ הַבָּא בְּשֵׁם יְהוָה בֵּרַכְנוּכֶם מִבֵּית יְהוָה ׃
BLESSED is the King that comes in the name of the LORD ··· LUKE ch 19 v. 38 ···

Post Script

THE ALMOND TREE

"And the word of the Lord came to me saying, "What do you see, Jeremiah?"
And I said, "I see a rod of an almond tree."
Then the Lord said to me,
"You have seen well, for I AM watching over My Word to perform it."

God keeps His word, His promises are true.

This meditation grew out of the remembrance of a vivid dream back in January 1980. It puzzled me. In the dream I was looking out over a panoramic view of hills and valleys. Closer to me, in the near foreground were some beautiful trees covered with pale pink blossom. They were glorious. In the middle and far distance there were more trees, but they were bare and wintry. This seemed strange to me. Why the contrast?

Then I saw a group of young people, boys and girls, in their late teens and early twenties. They were all dressed in white and were running up the hill towards where I was standing. They appeared to be running away and were very frightened. I looked more carefully to see why, and realised that beyond the horizon, towering up in to the sky, was a glorious translucent, shimmering emerald green wave. This tsunami wave was awe-inspiring and seemed to be suspended in the heavens and about to descend over the entire landscape.

I found myself calling out as I ran to meet them: "Don't be afraid, you'll get wet but you won't drown, you will be able to breath." I joined them and together we ran up the hill away from the wave. The water did indeed come down over us and we could breath.

The next thing I knew, I was in a vaguely familiar building, rather like the enormous entrance hall of All Nations Christian College, which I had recently left following two years' study. It was a bit different though, as the walls were now wood panelled. This seemed significant.

There were quite a few others there. A former fellow student (who had served as head student) saw me and came over. I found myself saying to him urgently, "With all this water around, hadn't we better turn off the electric lights?"
Then I woke up!

What a strange and powerful dream! There _____ now a little who might help: so we arranged to meet. She _____ almond trees, because they are the first to bloom in Israel in _____ while all the rest of the trees are still bare. Further research _____ rees feature in the Hebrew Scriptures as symbols of spiritual a_____ od that budded, flowered and fruited overnight; in the Tabern_____ en branched lamp stand incorporated design elements based on t_____ lowers of the almond tree; In later years, when called to be prophe_____ ous nation, the young Jeremiah was shown a picture of an almond ro_____, and the Lord reassured him that HE, the Lord was watching over His _____ perform it. It was a pun, because in Hebrew, the words for almond and wa_____ or guard look and sound very similar; in fact, the almond tree is called 'The Watcher."

This dream has stayed with me; it has been drawn and written down. In recent months, for a couple of years, in fact, it has returned to mind. It occurred to me that it could be explored in the context of the First and Second Coming of Messiah and worked on for a visual meditation: part of a series of visual biblical meditations begun back in the 1990s and earlier. This meditative drawing is the result.

Key thoughts:

*The Door open in heaven reveals another world that is the true one, the Reality of which this life is like a shadow. Jesus is the Door.
*We can see the Almond Tree in heaven and on earth. The shape is like a Menorah, the lamp stand in the Tabernacle. Jesus said 'I AM the Light of the world' during one of the festivals at a time when great ceremonial lamp stands were lit in the Temple courts. *The winged forms in the sky speak of Psalm 91: of God's protection and of the Holy Spirit as He broods over all Creation.

* The scripture verses woven in and among these wings remind us that through all time and beyond, our Creator God has been weaving together His plan to make, take and redeem a people from bondage and bring forth from them a Saviour to bless the whole world and save it from destruction, death and decay to give the gift of eternal life. From the very beginning it was in Father God's heart to rescue us all through the descendants of the Patriarchs: Abraham, Isaac and Jacob.

* The genealogies are part of this and were incorporated into the design. The verse from Hebrews 10 and Psalm 40 sums it all up: "A body Thou hast prepared for Me." This looks prophetically to Jesus who is the promised rescuer/redeemer for the whole of humanity.
See Psalm 139: "Behold I am fearfully and wonderfully made...woven together in my mother's womb.." writes David, youngest son of Jesse, descendant of Boaz of the tribe of Judah. David was a despised shepherd boy destined to be a great king, and to be ancestor of the King of Kings: the Messiah. It was prophesied that there would always be a descendant of David upon the throne. David was descended from the patriarchs: Abraham, Isaac and Jacob and the tribe of Judah, which

means "Prai[se]... [Jos]eph and Mary (Miriam in the Hebrew) were descendants [of King] David.

* The town of [Bet]hle[hem] in Judah where Jesus was born was prophesied as being the p[la]ce of [the] Messiah's birth. Bethlehem means House of Bread, (Jesu[s sai]d "I [am th]e bread of life.")
*The shepher[ds] under [the a]lmond tree represent the Patriarchs, (all three were shepherds), [and] a shepherd representing David can be seen running ahead of the o[the]rs to reach the stable door to see the 'Greater Son' that he was [p]art of making. "A body Thou hast prepared for Me."

*The figures in white are my young people from the dream and represent to me those of this new up and coming generation who are hungry for the living bread and looking for the Door to Life with a capital L. they too are descendants of the Patriarchs and have a death-defying role to play in God's plan for the end of the Ages.

*To the left in the corner is a myrtle tree. This speaks of redemption and restoration of the garden relationship with the Creator for all of His creation. Myrtle is also used symbolically at weddings and funerals, representing success and immortality and mysteries to be revealed. (Isaiah 55 and Zechariah 1).

*In anticipation of the joy to come, the Almond tree sheds its blossom over the whole scene, like confetti at a wedding.
*Take another look and see that the whole scene is embroidered on a square pouch. It reminds us of the High priest's breastplate that was worn over the heart as he served the Lord God in the tabernacle and Temple. It contained two stones called the "Lights and Perfections" which were used in making judgements. Jesus is our Great high priest who will never die. He ever lives to make intercession for us. He carries us in His heart.

*In the days just before He would give His life for the world on a Cross outside the city walls of Jerusalem, Jesus looked out over the city from the Mount of Olives and wept as He prophesied the terrible things that would happen there. But there was also hope as He promised that one day, when she, the City of Jerusalem, cries out, "Blessed is He Who comes in the name of the Lord," something called true Shalom (Peace) would happen. She would be acknowledging Him as the true Messiah, the One God has promised from the beginning.

*The Stable Door is a recurring theme in the series. In a famous children's story called "The Last Battle" the author, CS Lewis, describes a battle at the end of time in the imaginary land of Narnia. The battle raged around a mysterious stable, which was very different on the inside, not at all what you would expect, very much larger, different altogether. 'Many were very fearful of it. Later, at the end of the story, Queen Lucy spoke of another stable door back in her own world:

"In our world, too, a stable once had something in it that was bigger than our whole world."

This is the paradox of Messiah Jesus, Son of David, Son of Man, Son of God, King of the Universe through Whom all things were made, yet born in a stable, unknown and un-recognised that First time of His Coming two thousand years ago. This paradox is at the heart of the meditation. May it bless you with joy and thanksgiving for God's most precious gift to all who will receive Him: Jesus, our Immanuel —God With Us.

December 2003   Christine

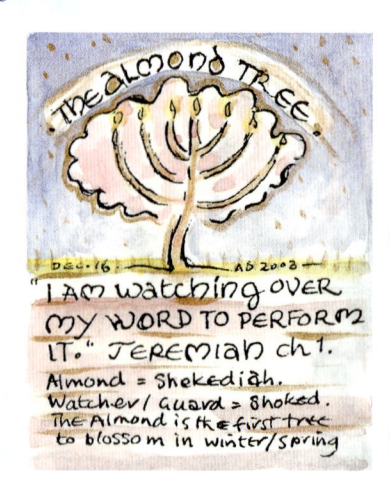

The almond tree
"I am watching over my word to perform it." Jeremiah ch 1.

Almond = Shekediah.
Watcher/Guard = Shoked.
The Almond is the first tree to blossom in winter/spring

Finally …
As you may have noticed, this last section was also written a while ago. These are thoughts along the Way. Something old, and something new, as I sat still and asked the Father:
'What next? What do you want me to see or hear… or 'sing' this year at Christmas?'

My hope and prayer is that you will use this book and make it your own, and that, in your busy life, you will make the time to 'walk and talk with the Father in the cool of the day' …in the garden of your life that the Father and you are creating!

May you sing the Father's Song with Him and give Him joy.
Christine M., Feast of Tabernacles 2012